S0-BCU-438

Property Of:
MAYWOOD PUBLIC
LIBRARY

# Dealing with CYBERBULLIES

By Drew Nelson

**Gareth Stevens**
Publishing

Please visit our website, www.garethstevens.com. For a free color catalog of all our high-quality books, call toll free 1-800-542-2595 or fax 1-877-542-2596.

**Library of Congress Cataloging-in-Publication Data**

Nelson, Drew, 1986-
Dealing with cyberbullies / Drew Nelson.
    p. cm. — (Cyberspace survival guide)
Includes index.
ISBN 978-1-4339-7221-8 (pbk.)
ISBN 978-1-4339-7222-5 (6-pack)
ISBN 978-1-4339-7220-1 (library binding)
1. Cyberbullying—Juvenile literature. 2. Bullying—Juvenile literature. 3. Internet and children—Juvenile literature. 4. Internet and teenagers—Juvenile literature. I. Title.
HV6773.15.C92N45 2013
302.34'3—dc23
                            2012006697

First Edition

Published in 2013 by
**Gareth Stevens Publishing**
111 East 14th Street, Suite 349
New York, NY 10003

Copyright © 2013 Gareth Stevens Publishing

Designer: Katelyn E. Reynolds
Editor: Therese M. Shea

Photo credits: Cover, p. 1 Thomas Grass/The Image Bank/Getty Images; cover, pp. 1, 3–24 (background) Gala/Shutterstock.com; cover, pp. 1, 3–24 (grunge banner; cursor graphics; search box graphic) Amgun/Shutterstock.com; p. 5 Jupiterimages/liquidlibrary/Thinkstock.com; p. 7 Hemera/Thinkstock.com; p. 8 Allison Long/Kansas City Star/MCT via Getty Images; pp. 11, 17, 19 iStockphoto/Thinkstock.com; p. 13 Chris Whitehead/Photodisc/Getty Images; p. 14 1000 Words/Shutterstock.com; p. 15 Brendan O'Sullivan/Photolibrary/Getty Images; p. 18 Hemera Technologies/Photos.com/Thinkstock.com; p. 21 Monkey Business Images/The Agency Collection/Getty Images; p. 23 ©iStockphoto.com/Stratol; p. 25 Bruce Laurance/The Image Bank/Getty Images; p. 27 Wendy Maeda/The Boston Globe via Getty Images; p. 28 ©iStockphoto.com/plherrera.

All rights reserved. No part of this book may be reproduced in any form without permission in writing from the publisher, except by a reviewer.

Printed in the United States of America

CPSIA compliance information: Batch #CS12GS: For further information contact Gareth Stevens, New York, New York at 1-800-542-2595.

# CONTENTS

Words in the glossary appear in **bold** type the first time they are used in the text.

# What Is BULLYING?

Bullying is a serious problem. There are different kinds of bullying, just as bullies can look different. Bullies may hurt people's bodies or their feelings. They may also try to scare or **embarrass** them. Bullying takes place over a period of time, not just once or twice. It's also done on purpose.

A third feature of bullying is that the bully is more powerful than the victim. Bullies may have more **physical** strength. They may be older or larger. Bullies may be in charge, or they may have more power over the other person in some other way. This power makes it hard for the victim to **defend** themselves.

 **Forms of Bullying**

Bullying can happen in many ways. It can be physical, like fighting, tripping, or pushing. It can be **verbal**, like name-calling and teasing. Bullying can be written, such as passing notes in school. Bullies can also use pictures or images to make someone feel bad.

A bully may focus on how someone is different, such as how they look or how they act.

5

# So What Is CYBERBULLYING?

Cyberbullying is when someone uses **technology**, such as cell phones and computers, to bully someone. Most of the time, it occurs on the Internet. It's a lot like other types of bullying that happen in person. It's usually meant to hurt, embarrass, or **threaten** someone.

Almost half of all American teenagers say they have been bullied online. It happens most to people who are at the end of middle school or in the beginning of high school. With technology becoming such a major part of young people's lives, reports of cyberbullying have been on the rise in recent years.

## 🔍 When Adults Cyberbully

The term "cyberbullying" applies to the behavior among people who are minors under the law, usually younger than 18. When cyberbullying takes place between adults or between an adult and a minor, it's called **harassment** or **stalking**. People can be sent to jail for cyber-harassment or cyber-stalking.

Technology helps young people keep in touch, but it also helps bullies spread their mean messages.

7

This girl was bullied because of a photo she posted online. However, she found a positive way to fight back.

Like other kinds of bullying, cyberbullying includes many types of behaviors. Sending mean e-mails and text messages to someone is cyberbullying. Another form is spreading lies or **rumors** about someone on the Internet. Other cyberbullies pretend to be someone else online to trick people into thinking the other person is a bully.

Although it may not seem like it, tricking someone into giving private **information** is considered cyberbullying, too. Posting others' photos online without permission may also be cyberbullying. So is making websites, videos, or fake **profiles** that are meant to cause hurt or embarrassment.

## 🔍 Sometimes It Takes Two . . .

In some cases of cyberbullying, one person is the bully and one person is the victim. In many other cases, people bully each other. The original victim may believe they're just defending themselves by responding in an unkind way. However, that means they're bullying, too.

# Being ANONYMOUS

Even though most people wouldn't consider themselves bullies, anyone can be a cyberbully. According to the Cyberbullying Research Center, at least one out of every five kids has bullied someone online at some point. One out of ten has been both the bully and the victim.

It's easy to be a cyberbully on the Internet because many sites allow people to remain anonymous. Anonymous means that no one knows who a person really is. Because of this, people say things online that they wouldn't normally say. People who are being mean think they can't get in trouble. This isn't true.

## 🔍 Tracking Them Down

Although people think they're anonymous on many Internet sites, they can be traced. Every computer has an address, called an IP address, that is recorded when information is sent or received online. Website operators can use this address to block people from using certain sites.

10

Even if you don't use your real name on a website, your computer's IP address is recorded.

11

# Where and When CYBERBULLYING HAPPENS

Regular bullying can only happen in places where people meet face-to-face. Cyberbullying can happen anywhere. Someone can get a text message or e-mail wherever they have their cell phone or an online connection. People get bullied in many different places on the Internet, including websites, instant messenger programs, and in chat rooms.

Cyberbullying can also happen any time, 24 hours a day and 7 days a week. The Internet doesn't close, like schools or parks do. Cyberbullying happens over the summer and on holidays. Sometimes, the person getting bullied doesn't know it until much later.

## 🔍 Direct or Indirect?

Cyberbullying can be divided into direct and indirect attacks. A direct attack is when someone sends a mean or threatening message straight to someone. In an indirect attack, the bully gets someone else to say or do mean things to someone for them, like telling someone to post a rumor online.

Unfortunately, technology has made
cyberbullying anytime and anywhere easy.

# Social Networking AND CYBERBULLIES

Social networking sites are websites that allow people to meet others and communicate with them using the Internet. People make profiles about themselves so other people can find and get to know them. Facebook, Myspace, Friendster, and Google+ are all social networking sites.

Social networking sites are common places for cyberbullying. Cyberbullying is easy on these sites because so many people belong to them. There are few rules about what people can say to each other. In some ways, making it effortless for people to connect with each other makes it easy for people to bully each other, too.

## Who Is Targeted?

Boys and girls are equally likely to be cyberbullied. Victims are often bullied in person and have other social problems, such as difficulty making friends and getting along with others. Fifteen-year-olds are more likely to be involved with cyberbullying than people of any other age.

Many social networking sites have rules that keep young people from joining them until they're 13 or 14 years old.

# Why Do PEOPLE BULLY?

If it makes so many people feel so bad, why would anyone become a cyberbully? According to the National Crime Prevention Council, four out of five teenagers believe that cyberbullies think their actions are funny.

The people asked also had many other ideas about why people might cyberbully. The cyberbullies may not think it's a big deal. Maybe they don't consider the consequences before they do it. Perhaps cyberbullies are encouraged by friends. Online bullies may think that everyone cyberbullies, and they're just trying to fit in. They might do it just because they don't think they'll get caught.

## For Everyone to See

Another big problem with cyberbullying is that most things are hard to keep private on the Internet. If a mean comment is posted on someone's Facebook page, all their friends can see it. If someone makes a website to embarrass someone, anyone who knows how to find it on the Internet can see it.

Before posting a teasing comment, people should think about how they would feel if someone said it about them.

# Profile of a Cyberbully

What does a cyberbully look or act like in real life? Boys and girls cyberbully the same amount. Cyberbullies are often kids who break rules and fight more often. Teenagers who cyberbully are more likely to say they're sad or lonely than other people. Also, most cyberbullies are older than their victims.

Everyone who spends time on the Internet should know how to spot a cyberbully.

The truth is that no one knows for sure what's going on in the minds of cyberbullies. They might be angry, upset, or looking for **revenge**. They might be bored and not think that what they're doing is mean. They might cyberbully to get attention if they don't have many friends.

Cyberbullies may have been bullied by someone else in person. They may bully people over the Internet to feel more powerful. All this really does, though, is hurt more people and teach them harmful ways to deal with their feelings. We can't know why cyberbullies act, but we do know how they make people feel.

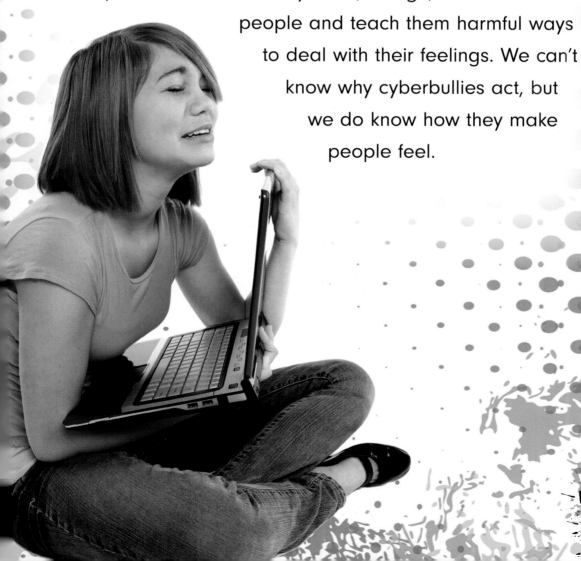

# The Effects of CYBERBULLYING

Cyberbullying may have a worse effect on victims than just making them feel embarrassed for a time. People who have been bullied online often avoid going to school. They may not want to face people who have read or seen things about them online. As a result, their grades go down. Victims are also more likely to have health problems and lower **self-esteem**.

People who are cyberbullied can have different kinds of problems in the future. They may turn to alcohol and drugs to help them feel better, which gets them into more trouble. Sadly, some young people have taken their own lives because of cyberbullying.

## 🔍 Bullying by Mistake

Sometimes, cyberbullying can begin as an accident. People may send a text message or e-mail to the wrong person by mistake. They might reveal something that was a secret. They also might not know that something is embarrassing for someone else. As the information continues to be passed around, cyberbullying may occur.

Bullying victims often feel alone, but most people know what it's like to be bullied. It's good to talk to people about it.

21

# Preventing CYBERBULLYING

Sometimes cyberbullying can be prevented. One easy way to keep from becoming a cyberbully is to think twice about posting or sending information electronically. This means being careful about pictures, possible secrets, or anything else that might hurt someone else. Once something is on the Internet, it may be hard to take off, especially if other people begin to forward it.

Using privacy settings on social networking accounts can also help prevent cyberbullying. Privacy settings allow the user to only share with people they know and trust. Other people can't see things that they aren't supposed to.

## 🔍 Signs of Cyberbullying

Many times, young people don't want to tell others they're being cyberbullied. They feel ashamed or embarrassed. Parents and friends should know the signs that someone is being cyberbullied. These include someone seeming upset after using the computer or cell phone, keeping secrets about online activities, and avoiding school activities.

# Account Settings

## Privacy Settings

## Log Out

## Help

Privacy settings should be changed to fit your needs.
Often when you first open a social networking
account, anyone can see your information.

# Stopping CYBERBULLYING

Even if cyberbullying has already started, there are a few ways to stop it before it gets any worse. One easy way is to not respond or react to the bully. Sometimes people are just mean to get another person to do something. If it doesn't work, the bully might stop.

However, if the bully continues, other people must get involved. A good first step is to talk to a trustworthy person. This could be an adult or a friend. They might have had the same thing happen to them, or they might know the bullies. They can help victims decide what to do. Sometimes, the school or even the police should be informed.

## 🔍 How Parents Can Help

Even though many adults don't have as much experience with technology as young people do, they have experience with bullying. They probably had to deal with bullying themselves and can give advice based on what happened. Just because some adults don't use Facebook doesn't mean they can't help with bullies.

Talking to parents about being cyberbullied can be helpful, but so can talking to teachers at school.

25

School counselors and principals can help with bullies and cyberbullies. In fact, many states have laws requiring school districts to have a plan to stop cyberbullying. Bullies may be punished at school. However, if the bullying is a threat to someone's life, the police will be called. In recent years, some cases of cyberbullying have resulted in young people paying fines or even going to jail.

Victims should save messages, posts, and texts from cyberbullies. These can be used later to prove that the person being bullied is telling the truth. Facing a cyberbully won't just help the person being bullied. It may also help others who are being bullied by the same person.

## 🔍 Cyber-Resources

There are many different websites that help young people deal with cyberbullying. *Stopcyberbullying.org* has a lot of information available for people of different ages. *Cyberbully411.org* is a site helping teenagers avoid cyberbullies and learn how to react to them in better ways.

Young people should share their experiences with cyberbullying. Pooling ideas and feelings can make victims feel stronger.

# What Can YOU DO TO HELP?

Even if you aren't the cyberbully or the victim, there are things you can do to prevent cyberbullying. You can refuse to pass along messages or rumors that could lead to people being hurt or embarrassed. People who say nothing while bullies hurt others are a part of the problem, too. You can tell friends to stop doing things that you think might hurt others. You can also report cyberbullying to an adult when you see it happening.

You could even work with friends, teachers, and others at school to make rules about cyberbullying. Together, you can raise awareness about cyberbullying in your community and online.

# Ways to React to Cyberbullying

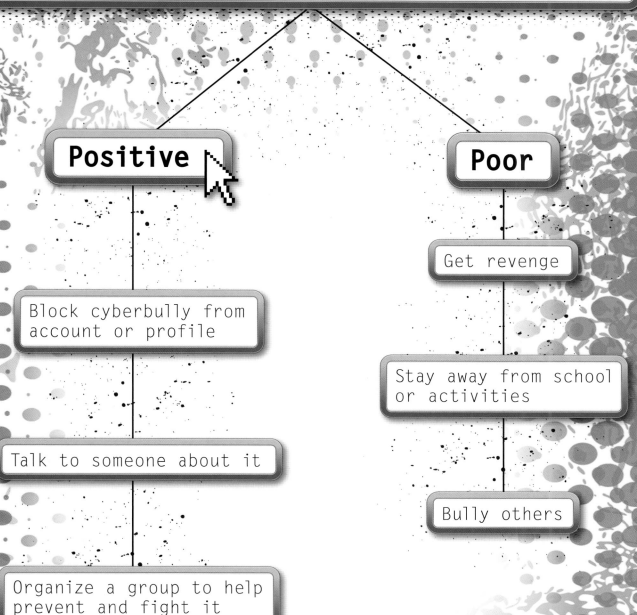

**Positive**

- Block cyberbully from account or profile
- Talk to someone about it
- Organize a group to help prevent and fight it

**Poor**

- Get revenge
- Stay away from school or activities
- Bully others

# GLOSSARY

**defend:** to keep safe from attack, harm, or danger

**embarrass:** to make someone uncomfortable or upset around other people

**harassment:** the act of creating an unpleasant or hostile situation by unwanted acts or words

**information:** facts and knowledge

**physical:** having to do with the body or body contact

**profile:** a collection of facts about someone, especially on a website

**revenge:** to punish someone in return for harm caused

**rumor:** a story passed around without facts to prove it

**self-esteem:** a person's belief in their own worth

**stalk:** to harass someone by constantly following or contacting them

**technology:** the use of machines and tools

**threaten:** to express a wish to harm someone

**verbal:** having to do with spoken words

# For More INFORMATION

## Books

Golus, Carrie. *Take a Stand! What You Can Do About Bullying*. Minneapolis, MN: Lerner Publications, 2009.

Hinduja, Sameer, and Justin W. Patchin. *Bullying Beyond the Schoolyard: Preventing and Responding to Cyberbullying*. Thousand Oaks, CA: Corwin Press, 2009.

Kowalski, Robin M., Susan P. Limber, and Patricia W. Agatston. *Cyberbullying: Bullying in the Digital Age*. Malden, MA: Wiley-Blackwell, 2012.

## Websites

### Prevent Cyberbullying and Internet Harassment
*cyberbully411.org*
This resource helps young people deal with cyberbullying and includes real-life stories of people who were bullied.

### Stop Cyberbullying
*www.stopcyberbullying.org*
Learn about how to react to cyberbullying and prevent your friends from becoming cyberbullies.

**Publisher's note to educators and parents:** Our editors have carefully reviewed these websites to ensure that they are suitable for students. Many websites change frequently, however, and we cannot guarantee that a site's future contents will continue to meet our high standards of quality and educational value. Be advised that students should be closely supervised whenever they access the Internet.

# INDEX